THIS
GENERATION

Living Life On Purpose

THE PLAYBOOK
VOLUME 1

DR. FREDERICK D. ACKLIN

ISBN: 978-1-965082-00-3

Publishing By: DemiCo National, LLC

www.DemiCoNational.com

TABLE OF CONTENTS

1. Understanding Your Identity in Christ   **Page 6**

- Knowing Who You Are in Christ

- Understanding Your Value and Worth

2. Discovering Your Purpose   **Page 10**

- Seeking God's Will for Your Life

- Identifying Your Spiritual Gifts and Talents

3. Overcoming Obstacles   **Page 14**

- Dealing with Doubt and Insecurities

- Handling Fear and Uncertainty

4. Developing a Kingdom Mindset   **Page 18**

- Aligning Your Thoughts with God's Word

- Cultivating a Heart of Service and Love

5. Walking in Faith   **Page 22**

- Trusting God's Plan for Your Life

- Stepping Out in Faith and Obedience

6. Building Kingdom Relationships   **Page 26**

- Surrounding Yourself with Positive Influences

- Serving Others and Building Community

7. Pursuing Excellence   **Page 30**

- Honoring God in Your Work and Endeavors

- Striving for Excellence in All You Do

8. Embracing Challenges   **Page 34**

- Seeing Trials as Opportunities for Growth

- Persevering in the Face of Adversity

9. Fulfilling Your Kingdom Potential   **Page 38**

- Living a Life of Purpose and Impact

- Leaving a Legacy for God's Kingdom

10. Reflecting on Your Journey   **Page 42**

- Moving Forward with Confidence and Purpose

PLAY 1

Understanding Your Identity in Christ

Understanding your identity in Christ is foundational to living a purposeful and fulfilling life as a believer. It involves knowing who you are in Christ and understanding your value and worth in God's eyes. When you accept Jesus Christ as your Savior, you become a new creation, adopted into God's family, and co-heir with Christ. This new identity shapes how you see yourself and how you relate to others.

Knowing who you are in Christ means recognizing that you are loved unconditionally by God. Your worth is not based on your achievements, appearance, or the opinions of others but on the fact that you are a beloved child of God. This realization brings a deep sense of security and confidence, knowing that you are accepted and valued by the Creator of the universe.

Understanding your value and worth in Christ also involves recognizing that you are created with a unique purpose and calling. God has endowed you with specific gifts, talents, and abilities to fulfill His plans for your life. By embracing your identity as a child of God, you can walk in confidence, knowing that you have a significant role to play in God's kingdom.

Moreover, when you understand your identity in Christ, you are no longer defined by your past mistakes, failures, or shortcomings. Instead, you are forgiven, redeemed, and made righteous through the blood of Jesus Christ. This freedom from guilt and shame allows you to live victoriously and to pursue God's purposes with boldness and faith.

By grounding your identity in Christ, you can navigate life's challenges with resilience and hope. When you face struggles, doubts, or criticisms, you can stand firm in the truth of who you are in Christ. This knowledge empowers you to overcome obstacles, persevere in trials, and live a life that glorifies God in all that you do.

In summary, understanding your identity in Christ is a transformative journey that shapes your self-perception, relationships, and life's purpose. It is a journey of discovering the depth of God's love for you, the value He places on your life, and the unique calling He has placed on you. Embracing your identity in Christ enables you to live authentically, confidently, and purposefully, as you fulfill the plans and purposes God has for you.

Write your understanding of your value and worth in Christ?

_____

_____

_____

_____

_____

_____

_____

_____

_____

_____

_____

_____

_____

PLAY 2

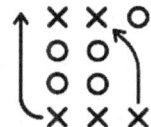

Discovering Your Purpose

Discovering your purpose is a crucial aspect of living a fulfilling and meaningful life as a Christian. It involves seeking God's will for your life and identifying the spiritual gifts and talents that He has bestowed upon you. By aligning yourself with God's plan and utilizing your unique gifts, you can walk in the fullness of your calling and make a significant impact in the world.

Seeking God's will for your life is a continuous journey of prayer, reflection, and obedience. It requires surrendering your desires and ambitions to God and allowing Him to guide your steps. Through reading the Bible, spending time in prayer, and seeking wise counsel, you can discern God's purposes for you and walk in alignment with His perfect plan.

Identifying your spiritual gifts and talents is another essential component of discovering your purpose. God has uniquely gifted each believer with specific abilities and talents to be used for His glory and the building up of the body of Christ. By recognizing and developing these gifts, you can serve others effectively, contribute to the advancement of God's kingdom, and experience fulfillment in your calling.

Understanding your purpose involves connecting your passions, skills, and opportunities with God's overarching plan for your life. As you explore your interests and strengths, seek feedback from others, and pray for discernment, you can uncover how God intends for you to use your gifts to serve Him and others. This process of self-discovery and discernment is essential for living a purpose-driven life.

By embracing your purpose and walking in alignment with God's will, you can experience a deep sense of fulfillment, joy, and peace. When you operate in the gifts and talents that God has given you, you can make a unique and valuable contribution to the world around you. Your life becomes a testimony to God's grace, wisdom, and power working through you for His glory.

In summary, discovering your purpose involves seeking God's will for your life, identifying your spiritual gifts and talents, and aligning yourself with His divine plan. It is a journey of self-discovery, prayer, and obedience that leads to a life of significance, impact, and fulfillment. As you walk in your God-given purpose, you can bring light, hope, and transformation to the world around you, reflecting the love and glory of God in all that you do.

What do you believe is God's will for your life? What are your spiritual gifts and talents?

_____

_____

_____

_____

_____

_____

_____

_____

_____

_____

_____

_____

_____

PLAY 3

Overcoming Obstacles

Overcoming obstacles is a common experience for believers on their journey of faith. Two significant challenges that Christians often face are dealing with doubt and insecurities, as well as handling fear and uncertainty. However, the Bible provides guidance and encouragement on how to navigate these obstacles with faith, courage, and reliance on God's strength.

Doubt and insecurities can hinder believers from stepping into their full potential and fulfilling their God-given purpose. The Bible reminds us to trust in the Lord with all our hearts and lean not on our own understanding (Proverbs 3:5). By focusing on God's promises, seeking His wisdom through prayer and studying His Word, we can overcome doubt and insecurities that may arise in our hearts and minds.

Fear and uncertainty are common emotions that can paralyze us and prevent us from moving forward in obedience to God's call. However, the Bible repeatedly encourages us not to fear, for God is with us and will strengthen and help us (Isaiah 41:10). By placing our trust in God's sovereignty and faithfulness, we can face our fears with courage and confidence, knowing that He is in control of all things.

When dealing with doubt and insecurities, it is essential to remember that our identity is rooted in Christ, not in our circumstances or feelings. We are reminded in Ephesians 2:10 that we are God's workmanship, created in Christ Jesus for good works that He has prepared in advance for us to do.

By embracing our identity as beloved children of God, we can find strength and confidence to overcome doubts and insecurities.

Similarly, when facing fear and uncertainty, we can find comfort in the promises of God's presence and faithfulness. Psalm 23:4 assures us that even though we walk through the valley of the shadow of death, we need not fear, for God is with us. By anchoring our faith in God's unchanging character and promises, we can face uncertain circumstances with peace and assurance.

In times of doubt, insecurities, fear, and uncertainty, the key is to turn to God in prayer, seeking His guidance, comfort, and strength. The Bible encourages us to cast all our anxieties on Him because He cares for us (1 Peter 5:7). Through prayer, meditation on Scripture, and fellowship with other believers, we can find the strength and courage to overcome obstacles and walk in faith.

In summary, overcoming obstacles such as doubt, insecurities, fear, and uncertainty is a vital aspect of the Christian journey. By relying on God's promises, seeking His guidance, and trusting in His faithfulness, believers can navigate challenges with confidence and hope. Through prayer, faith, and obedience to God's Word, we can overcome obstacles and grow in our relationship with Him, ultimately experiencing His peace, presence, and power in our lives.

How do you deal with doubt and insecurities?

_____

_____

_____

_____

_____

_____

PLAY 4

Developing a Kingdom Mindset

Developing a Kingdom mindset is essential for believers seeking to live a life that aligns with God's purposes and values. It involves aligning your thoughts with God's Word and cultivating a heart of service and love towards others. By focusing on these aspects, Christians can grow spiritually, impact their communities, and bring glory to God through their lives.

Aligning your thoughts with God's Word is foundational to developing a Kingdom mindset. The Bible teaches that believers should renew their minds and not conform to the patterns of this world but be transformed by the renewing of their minds (Romans 12:2). By immersing ourselves in Scripture, meditating on God's truths, and allowing His Word to shape our thinking, we can develop a mindset that reflects His wisdom, love, and values.

Cultivating a heart of service and love is another key aspect of developing a Kingdom mindset. Jesus taught that the greatest commandments are to love the Lord your God with all your heart, soul, and mind, and to love your neighbor as yourself (Matthew 22:37-39). By following Jesus' example of selfless service and sacrificial love, believers can demonstrate the Kingdom values of compassion, humility, and generosity in their interactions with others.

A Kingdom mindset prioritizes God's kingdom agenda over personal desires and ambitions. It involves seeking first the Kingdom of God and His righteousness, trusting that all other things will be provided by God (Matthew 6:33). By aligning our hearts with God's purposes and seeking to advance His kingdom on earth, we can live with a sense of purpose, direction, and fulfillment.

Developing a Kingdom mindset also involves embracing humility and servant leadership, following the example of Jesus who came not to be served but to serve (Mark 10:45). By humbly serving others, putting their needs above our own, and seeking to make a positive impact in their lives, we reflect the heart of Christ and demonstrate the values of the Kingdom.

In cultivating a Kingdom mindset, believers are called to be salt and light in the world, influencing others through their words, actions, and attitudes (Matthew 5:13-16). By living out Kingdom principles of love, justice, and mercy in their daily lives, Christians can be a powerful witness to the transformative power of God's grace and truth.

In summary, developing a Kingdom mindset involves aligning your thoughts with God's Word, cultivating a heart of service and love, and living out the values of the Kingdom in your daily life. By immersing yourself in Scripture, embracing a lifestyle of selfless service, and reflecting the love of Christ in all that you do, you can impact your world for God's glory and contribute to the advancement of His Kingdom on earth.

Write your story of faith and following God.

_____

_____

_____

_____

_____

_____

_____

_____

_____

PLAY 5

Walking in Faith

Walking in faith is a fundamental aspect of the Christian journey, requiring believers to trust God's plan for their lives and step out in faith and obedience. By placing their confidence in God's sovereignty and following His leading with obedience, Christians can experience spiritual growth, divine guidance, and the fulfillment of God's purposes in their lives.

Trusting God's plan for your life involves acknowledging that God's ways are higher than our ways and His thoughts are higher than our thoughts (Isaiah 55:8-9). It requires surrendering our desires, fears, and uncertainties to God and resting in His providence and wisdom. By placing our trust in God's perfect plan and timing, we can walk confidently in the assurance that He is working all things together for our good (Romans 8:28).

Stepping out in faith and obedience is a demonstration of trust in God's faithfulness and promises. The Bible is filled with examples of individuals who stepped out in faith and obedience, even when the path ahead seemed uncertain or challenging. Abraham's willingness to leave his homeland and follow God's call (Genesis 12:1-4) and Peter's bold step of faith to walk on water towards Jesus (Matthew 14:28-29) are just a few examples of individuals who exemplified faith and obedience.

Walking in faith requires courage, perseverance, and a willingness to take risks for the sake of God's kingdom. Hebrews 11:6 reminds us that without faith, it is impossible to please God, for whoever would draw near to God must believe that He exists and that He rewards those who seek Him. By stepping out in faith and obedience, believers demonstrate their trust in God's character and their willingness to follow His leading wherever it may lead.

While walking in faith may involve stepping into the unknown and facing challenges, believers can take comfort in the assurance that God is with them every step of the way. Joshua 1:9 encourages us to be strong and courageous, not to be afraid or discouraged, for the Lord our God is with us wherever we go. By relying on God's presence, strength, and guidance, believers can navigate life's uncertainties with confidence and peace.

Walking in faith also involves a deepening relationship with God through prayer, meditation on Scripture, and fellowship with other believers. By seeking God's will, listening for His voice, and obeying His commands, believers can grow in their faith, experience spiritual transformation, and witness the miraculous work of God in their lives.

In summary, walking in faith requires trusting God's plan for your life, stepping out in faith and obedience, and relying on His strength and guidance. By surrendering to God's will, following His leading with courage and obedience, and seeking to grow in intimacy with Him, believers can experience the abundant life and fulfillment that comes from walking in faith. As they trust in God's promises and step out in obedience, they can witness the power of God at work in their lives and bring glory to His name.

Who are the positive influences in your life and what purposes do they serve?

_____

_____

_____

_____

_____

_____

PLAY 6

Building Kingdom Relationships

Building Kingdom Relationships is a fundamental aspect emphasized in the Bible, highlighting the importance of surrounding oneself with positive influences and serving others to foster a sense of community. In the Scriptures, individuals are encouraged to be mindful of the company they keep, as it can shape their beliefs, behaviors, and ultimately their destinies. Proverbs 13:20 states, "Walk with the wise and become wise, for a companion of fools suffers harm," underscoring the significance of choosing companions who uplift and inspire one to grow spiritually and morally.

Additionally, serving others is a core principle in the Christian faith, exemplified by Jesus Christ Himself, who came not to be served but to serve (Matthew 20:28). By following His example, believers are called to demonstrate humility, compassion, and selflessness in their interactions with others, thus building a strong sense of community rooted in love and mutual support. Galatians 5:13 reinforces this notion, stating, "Serve one another humbly in love," emphasizing the transformative power of service in nurturing meaningful relationships.

Furthermore, the concept of building Kingdom relationships extends beyond personal interactions to encompass the broader community of believers. In Romans 12:4-5, the apostle Paul likens the body of Christ to a single organism with diverse parts working together harmoniously, highlighting the interconnectedness and interdependence among believers. This metaphor underscores the importance of collaboration, mutual support, and unity in fostering a thriving community that reflects God's love and grace to the world.

Moreover, the Bible emphasizes the significance of forgiveness and reconciliation in maintaining healthy Kingdom relationships. In Matthew 6:14-15, Jesus teaches the disciples the importance of forgiving others as they have been forgiven by God, underscoring the transformative power of forgiveness in healing wounds, restoring relationships, and fostering unity within the community. By practicing forgiveness and reconciliation, believers can overcome conflicts, build trust, and cultivate a culture of grace and mercy within the Kingdom community.

Additionally, the Bible encourages believers to prioritize love and compassion in their interactions with others, as exemplified by the greatest commandment to love God with all one's heart, soul, and mind, and to love one's neighbor as oneself (Matthew 22:37-39). By embodying love and compassion in their relationships, believers can create a nurturing and supportive environment where individuals feel valued, accepted, and encouraged to grow in their faith and character.

In conclusion, Building Kingdom Relationships from a biblical perspective involves surrounding oneself with positive influences, serving others, and fostering a sense of community rooted in love, humility, and mutual support. By following the teachings and examples set forth in the Scriptures, believers can cultivate meaningful connections, promote unity, and reflect God's love and grace in their interactions with others. Through intentional efforts to build Kingdom relationships, individuals can experience spiritual growth, emotional healing, and a profound sense of belonging within the community of faith, ultimately glorifying God and advancing His Kingdom on earth.

Do you work with a spirit of excellence? If not, what is hindering you from improving your performance?

PLAY 7

Pursuing Excellence

Pursuing Excellence involves honoring God in all aspects of one's work and endeavors and striving for excellence as a reflection of one's commitment to serving Him wholeheartedly. Colossians 3:23-24 underscores the importance of working diligently and with excellence, stating, "Whatever you do, work at it with all your heart, as working for the Lord, not for human masters...It is the Lord Christ you are serving." This verse emphasizes the significance of honoring God through one's work by giving one's best effort and maintaining a standard of excellence in all tasks.

Moreover, the Bible encourages believers to pursue excellence in all they do as a means of glorifying God and fulfilling their calling to be His ambassadors on earth. 1 Corinthians 10:31 instructs, "So whether you eat or drink or whatever you do, do it all for the glory of God," reminding believers that even the smallest actions can be done in a spirit of excellence to honor and magnify God's name. By approaching every task with a mindset of dedication, integrity, and excellence, individuals can demonstrate their commitment to serving God with their whole being.

Furthermore, pursuing excellence from a biblical perspective involves recognizing and developing the talents and gifts that God has bestowed upon each individual. In the parable of the talents (Matthew 25:14-30), Jesus teaches the importance of stewarding one's abilities well and maximizing them for the Kingdom's advancement. By investing time, effort, and resources in developing one's skills and talents, believers can fulfill their potential and contribute meaningfully to God's work on earth.

Additionally, the pursuit of excellence in one's work and endeavors is closely tied to the biblical principle of stewardship. Believers are called to be faithful stewards of the resources, opportunities, and responsibilities entrusted to them by God, using them wisely and effectively for His purposes. In Luke 16:10, Jesus affirms the significance of faithful stewardship, stating, "Whoever can be trusted with very little can also be trusted with much, and whoever is dishonest with very little will also be dishonest with much."

Moreover, pursuing excellence from a biblical perspective involves cultivating a spirit of perseverance, resilience, and determination in the face of challenges and setbacks. James 1:2-4 encourages believers to consider trials as opportunities for growth and refinement, stating, "Consider it pure joy, my brothers and sisters, whenever you face trials of many kinds, because you know that the testing of your faith produces perseverance." By embracing challenges as opportunities to grow in character and faith, individuals can develop a spirit of excellence that is steadfast, unwavering, and resilient in the pursuit of God's purposes.

In conclusion, pursuing excellence from a biblical perspective entail honoring God in one's work and endeavors, striving for excellence as a reflection of one's commitment to serving Him wholeheartedly, and maximizing the talents and gifts entrusted by God. By approaching every task with diligence, integrity, and a spirit of stewardship, believers can glorify God in all they do, fulfill their calling as His ambassadors, and contribute meaningfully to His Kingdom's advancement. Through perseverance, resilience, and a commitment to excellence, individuals can demonstrate their devotion to serving God with excellence in every aspect of their lives, bringing honor and glory to His name.

Who do you become when adversity presents itself?

_____

_____

PLAY 8

Embracing Challenges

Embracing challenges involves seeing trials as opportunities for growth and persevering in the face of adversity, trusting in God's sovereignty and faithfulness. James 1:2-4 encourages believers to consider trials as a reason for joy, as they produce perseverance and refine one's faith. By viewing challenges through a lens of faith, individuals can cultivate a mindset that embraces difficulties as opportunities for spiritual growth, character development, and a deeper reliance on God's strength and guidance.

Furthermore, the Bible teaches that adversity can lead to the development of perseverance, resilience, and endurance in the face of trials. Romans 5:3-4 affirms this notion, stating, "Not only so, but we also glory in our sufferings, because we know that suffering produces perseverance; perseverance, character; and character, hope." By enduring challenges with faith and perseverance, believers can develop a steadfast and unwavering spirit that reflects their trust in God's providence and promises.

Moreover, embracing challenges from a biblical perspective involves seeking God's wisdom, strength, and guidance in navigating difficult circumstances. Proverbs 3:5-6 advises believers to trust in the Lord with all their hearts and lean not on their understanding, acknowledging God in all their ways so that He may direct their paths. By relying on God's wisdom and strength, individuals can persevere through adversity with confidence, knowing that He is with them every step of the way, guiding and sustaining them through the storm.

Additionally, the Bible teaches that God uses challenges and trials to refine and purify the faith of believers, shaping them into vessels fit for His purposes. 1 Peter 1:6-7 emphasizes this truth, stating, "In all this you greatly rejoice, though now for a little while you may have had to suffer grief in all kinds of trials. These have come so that the proven genuineness of your faith—of greater worth than gold, which perishes even though refined by fire—may result in praise, glory, and honor when Jesus Christ is revealed." By embracing challenges as opportunities for spiritual refinement, believers can grow in faith, character, and resilience, ultimately bringing glory to God through their perseverance.

Furthermore, the Bible encourages believers to remain steadfast in their faith and hope, even in the midst of trials and tribulations. Hebrews 10:35-36 exhorts believers not to throw away their confidence, for it will be richly rewarded, and to persevere so that when they have done the will of God, they will receive what He has promised. By holding fast to their faith and hope in God's promises, individuals can weather the storms of life with courage, perseverance, and unwavering trust in His faithfulness.

In conclusion, embracing challenges from a biblical perspective involves seeing trials as opportunities for growth, persevering in the face of adversity, and trusting in God's sovereignty and faithfulness. By viewing challenges through a lens of faith, seeking God's wisdom and strength, and remaining steadfast in their faith and hope, believers can navigate difficult circumstances with resilience, perseverance, and unwavering trust in God's providence and promises. Through trials and tribulations, individuals have the opportunity to grow in faith, character, and resilience, ultimately bringing glory to God through their perseverance and unwavering trust in His unfailing love and grace.

Who do you become when adversity presents itself?

PLAY 9

Fulfilling Your Kingdom Potential

Fulfilling Your Kingdom Potential from a biblical perspective involves living a life of purpose and impact, striving to leave a lasting legacy that glorifies God and advances His Kingdom on earth. Ephesians 2:10 affirms that believers are created in Christ Jesus to do good works, which God prepared in advance for them to do. This verse emphasizes the importance of living a purpose-driven life, using one's gifts, talents, and resources to make a positive impact on others and fulfill God's plan for their lives.

Moreover, the Bible encourages believers to be intentional about leaving a legacy that reflects their commitment to serving God and His Kingdom. Proverbs 13:22 states, "A good person leaves an inheritance for their children's children, but a sinner's wealth is stored up for the righteous," highlighting the significance of leaving a spiritual legacy of faith, values, and virtues that endure beyond one's lifetime. By investing in relationships, sharing the gospel, and living out one's faith authentically, individuals can leave a lasting legacy that inspires future generations to follow Christ and impact the world for His glory.

Furthermore, fulfilling your Kingdom potential involves using your God-given gifts and talents to serve others and make a difference in the world. 1 Peter 4:10-11 encourages believers to use their gifts to serve others, faithfully administering God's grace in its various forms, so that in all things God may be praised through Jesus Christ. By leveraging their unique abilities and talents for the benefit of others, individuals can fulfill their Kingdom potential and contribute meaningfully to the advancement of God's purposes on earth.

Additionally, the Bible teaches that believers are called to be salt and light in the world, influencing others positively and pointing them towards God's love and truth. In Matthew 5:13-16, Jesus declares that believers are the salt of the earth and the light of the world, encouraging them to let their light shine before others, so that they may see their good deeds and glorify their Father in heaven. By living out their faith boldly and authentically, individuals can fulfill their Kingdom potential by impacting others and drawing them closer to God.

Moreover, fulfilling your Kingdom potential involves seeking first the Kingdom of God and His righteousness, trusting that all other things will be added unto you (Matthew 6:33). By prioritizing God's Kingdom over worldly pursuits and trusting in His provision and guidance, believers can live a life of purpose, impact, and fulfillment, knowing that their ultimate goal is to glorify God and advance His Kingdom on earth.

In conclusion, fulfilling your Kingdom potential from a biblical perspective entails living a life of purpose and impact, leaving a legacy that glorifies God and advances His Kingdom, using your gifts and talents to serve others and make a difference in the world, being salt and light in the world, and seeking first the Kingdom of God in all things. By embracing these principles and aligning your life with God's purposes, you can fulfill your Kingdom potential, make a lasting impact for eternity, and leave a legacy that honors God and inspires others to follow Him wholeheartedly.

What do you believe to be your purpose? How does that purpose impact the world around you?

_____

_____

_____

_____

PLAY 10

Reflecting on Your Journey

Reflecting on Your Journey involves looking back on the path you have walked, acknowledging God's faithfulness, and learning from both the victories and challenges you have encountered. Psalm 77:11-12 declares, "I will remember the deeds of the Lord; yes, I will remember your miracles of long ago. I will consider all your works and meditate on all your mighty deeds," emphasizing the importance of reflecting on God's past faithfulness as a source of encouragement and strength for the future.

As you reflect on your journey, it is crucial to move forward with confidence and purpose, trusting in God's guidance and provision for the road ahead. Proverbs 3:5-6 instructs believers to trust in the Lord with all their hearts and lean not on their understanding, acknowledging Him in all their ways so that He may direct their paths. By surrendering to God's leading and relying on His wisdom, individuals can move forward with confidence, knowing that He is in control of their future and will guide them in fulfilling His purposes.

Furthermore, reflecting on your journey from a biblical perspective involves seeking God's perspective on your past experiences, both the joys and the trials. Romans 8:28 assures believers that all things work together for good for those who love God and are called according to His purpose, indicating that even the challenges and hardships encountered along the journey have a purpose in God's greater plan. By trusting in God's sovereignty and providence, individuals can move forward with confidence, knowing that He can redeem every experience for His glory and their growth.

Additionally, the Bible encourages believers to press on toward the goal, forgetting what is behind and straining toward what is ahead (Philippians 3:13-14). By focusing on the future with faith, determination, and a sense of purpose, individuals can overcome setbacks, disappointments, and distractions that may hinder their progress, moving forward with confidence in God's promises and provision.

Moreover, reflecting on your journey from a biblical perspective involves embracing a spirit of gratitude for God's faithfulness, provision, and blessings along the way. Psalm 136:1 declares, "Give thanks to the Lord, for he is good. His love endures forever," reminding believers to cultivate a heart of thanksgiving for all that God has done in their lives. By expressing gratitude for God's faithfulness and provision, individuals can move forward with confidence, knowing that He will continue to guide them and fulfill His promises in their lives.

In conclusion, reflecting on your journey from a biblical perspective entail looking back on the path you have walked, moving forward with confidence and purpose, trusting in God's guidance and provision, seeking His perspective on past experiences, and embracing a spirit of gratitude for His faithfulness. By integrating these principles into your life, you can navigate the journey ahead with faith, determination, and a sense of purpose, knowing that God is with you every step of the way, guiding, strengthening, and empowering you to fulfill His purposes and glorify His name.

What is the commitment you need to make to yourself that will enable you to live the life God has for you?

_____

_____

_____

_____